# Our *Beautiful* Babies Dear

# Our Beautiful Babies Dear

*Enduring the Loss of Miscarriage*

LINDSEY SALLOWAY

iUniverse, Inc.
Bloomington

**Our Beautiful Babies Dear**
**Enduring the Loss of Miscarriage**



*iUniverse books may be ordered through booksellers or by contacting:*

*iUniverse*
*1663 Liberty Drive*
*Bloomington, IN 47403*
*www.iuniverse.com*
*1-800-Authors (1-800-288-4677)*



*ISBN: 978-1-4759-9380-6 (sc)*
*ISBN: 978-1-4759-9382-0 (hc)*
*ISBN: 978-1-4759-9381-3 (ebk)*

*Library of Congress Control Number: 2013910219*

*Printed in the United States of America*

*iUniverse rev. date: 06/10/2013*

To our three children and our nephew,
who are playing together forever.

We had you for a short time
But not for very long,
And every single day since,
In my heart you are a song—

A song of what I miss most,
And what I wish I'd known,
Your hands, your feet, your little face
And how you would have grown;

A song of what we could have had,
The family we should have been,
Something I will always want,
but will always be a dream.

A song that says you love us,
And know that we love you;
It says that this will never change,
It will always be real and true.

But now you are in heaven,
And your song is heard loud and clear;
We'll treasure that song forever more,
Our beautiful babies dear.

# Preface

If you've picked this up and have turned to this page, chances are you have recently suffered a miscarriage. It may be your second, your third, or your tenth. Maybe you know someone who has had one, and you are hoping to find that perfect book that will help to pull her out of her misery through tales of other women who have suffered but have maintained hope because of their positive beliefs and attitudes. This is not that book. It is a bit bitter, slightly cynical, and entirely selfish on my part. It is a simple attempt by a woman who has just suffered her third miscarriage in ten months to distract herself and, maybe, feel a little bit better.

It started out as a sort of diary, because I wanted to make sure that when I came out of my fog, I had something to turn to, to help me remember this time in my life. Then it started to transform into a hate letter toward people who didn't offer me the support I needed. And it became a love letter to those who did. Eventually, the hateful thoughts made their way out of it altogether. I realized that by offering those people my attention I was still giving them as much of me as the supportive bunch were getting, and that didn't seem fair.

I wrote this over the course of about two years, and you'll notice that some of it is written in the present tense, when I am actually going through certain things. At other times, it is written long after that particular phase or happening occurred. I didn't set out to write a book, and I didn't give myself a certain time frame. I wrote when I felt I needed to write.

I can't promise a happy ending to your story. I can't guarantee that you will end up carrying a child to full term. I'm not sure what your personal trip will be or whether it will be the same as mine. Maybe you will be like the majority of women who suffer a miscarriage and, after the one, go on to have a perfectly healthy child. This is not the case for all women, though. It wasn't the case for me, which is partly what led me to write this book. After looking for books myself that wouldn't fill me with false hope and leave me feeling bitter toward the writer, I decided to write the story on my own. Please just take this book for what it is: an honest look at miscarriage and the journey that some women end up taking on the path to being a mom.

# Introduction

As I type this, it is January 7, 2013, and I am 29 years old. This is the year that I will turn 30, the year that my husband, Tosh, and I will celebrate seven years together and three years of marriage.

I grew up in Penticton, British Columbia, born into a family that already had two girls, my beautiful sisters, Chelsey and Courtney. While my sisters and I didn't always see eye to eye (our parents used to threaten divorce if we couldn't figure out how to live in relative peace and harmony), we are best friends today. Chelsey, the eldest of the three Hobbs girls, is a typical oldest child. Quiet and reserved, thoughtful and caring, she always wants everyone to have the perfect life and never suffer heartache of any kind. Courtney, the middle child, is, in a word, silly. She loves life. She sets out to have a good time and, with an easy-going, laid-back attitude, that is just what she does. She is also fiercely loyal and protective and has had my back on more than one occasion.

Then there's me, the baby. I'm the loud one in the family, without question. I'm also the obstinate, stubborn, annoyingly principled, just a little bit "out-there" one in the family. In other words, I'm the quintessential baby.

I was very fortunate to have grown up in a loving family. Our parents were (and still are) fantastic examples, and I've tried to model myself after them. No, we weren't perfect, by any means, but we had it pretty good. We were fortunate that we didn't ever have to suffer huge heartaches or tragedies when we were young. As we grew older and my sisters and I left Penticton for Calgary, we became very close, and we are truly best friends now.

Tosh came into the picture seven years ago, on January 25 (his birthday). We met at a pub one night, while my cousin and I were visiting my sister, who worked there. When I took off on him (because Courtney needed a ride to the hospital as a result of an oncoming bladder infection), he was certain it was an excuse to get away from him. That's why I had to call him a few days later—and now we're coming up to seven years. Again, as with my early life experiences, my time with Tosh has been pretty free of catastrophe. My grandpa passed away a few days after Tosh and I went on our first date. We've had family members die, a couple suffer from cancer, and a few other heartaches along the way, but for the most part, our relationship has been pretty easy.

Tosh is an amazing person. He is more intelligent than he will ever give himself credit for. He has a sense of humour that, even at the absolute worst of times, doesn't waver in the slightest. To Tosh, life is the time we are allotted to have fun, enjoy the things we love to do, and embrace every minute to the fullest.

Over our time together, we have both completed our post-secondary educations: I have a journalism degree, and Tosh is a journeyman electrician. We've bought our first and second home, travelled as often as possible, and adopted three wonderful dogs into our family. Cleo, Talli, and Zeus are, in short, our children. They are all rescue dogs, all adopted as adorable puppies, and Tosh and I love them more than anything.

# Let's Have a Baby

Tosh and I were married on July 17, 2010. It was a beautiful, albeit scorching hot, day in the Okanagan Valley. We had a small wedding, with just our closest family and friends. The ceremony was short and sweet, and the reception was just what we had imagined—a great party with the people we loved.

Being 26 when we married, we were one of the last couples in our group to take the plunge. Before our big day, we extensively discussed children, and we decided that there was absolutely no way we would have children or even attempt to get pregnant in our first year of marriage. All our other married friends had gotten pregnant before their first anniversary, and we didn't want to follow the trend. That's not to say it is a bad thing to have kids right away; it just wasn't for us. Things are different now. Couples date a lot longer before they are married (Tosh and I were together for four and a half years before we said I do). They live together and, in the case of most of the couples we know, already own houses. So, it is the natural progression of events to marry and start having kids right after your walk down the aisle. Having just bought a house and a puppy the year before we were married, we felt that that was enough for the time being. We were going to travel, save money, and enjoy ourselves a bit before being tied down to children.

All of our plans changed a short three months later, when my wonderful friend Terri took her own walk down the aisle. Tosh and I learned that day that when you are at a wedding, things happen to you. The singles find themselves desiring that feeling of falling in love, the unmarried couples have a sudden urge to be as blissfully joined for life as the bride and groom are, and apparently, the married-and-childless suddenly want to be married with children. So that was how we immediately went from being a we'll-wait-a-year-or-two couple to being a let's-have-a-baby-right-now couple.

Shortly after Christmas 2010, I went to the doctor to have a physical, just to make sure that I was in good health and okay to try to conceive. The doctor did a quick internal exam and, lo and behold, saw something that he thought indicated the possible beginnings of a pregnancy.

I—often to my own detriment—have a *very* overactive imagination. I also have an uncanny ability to convince myself of nearly anything. If I were ever part of a pharmaceutical test, I would definitely be the patient who the placebo worked for. My husband actually jokes that I have the most powerful mind in the world when it comes to convincing myself of things.

I told my family that my doctor thought I was pregnant. I stopped drinking coffee and alcohol immediately; I also stopped eating processed meat, unpasteurized milk products, and anything else that I had heard might harm a growing baby.

A few days after my appointment (and the day before my period was due), off I went to get a dreaded blood test. Yes, even at my age I'm *terrified* of needles! For a girl who tends to faint at the thought of giving blood, I thought I did pretty well. I lay down, which I have to do for all blood tests, counted backward from 10, stayed lying down for a few minutes, and then dragged myself up and out of the lab—feeling rather proud of myself for being such a tough cookie. Then I fainted in the elevator on the way down to the first floor. Well, of course, my overactive mind began to wonder what would happen to the possible little fetus developing inside me as a result of this fainting spell. I hounded my doctor's poor receptionist until my blood results came in.

That was my first mistake. While I did have slight levels of hCG in my blood, the levels were too low to be considered a viable pregnancy. What I had would later be referred to as a "chemical" pregnancy.

So, if I am going to provide any tips at all, here is tip #1: Even when actively trying to get pregnant, don't jump the gun on testing. Wait until you have missed your period by a couple of days.

Chemical pregnancies are rather common, and you only set yourself up for heartbreak if you see a positive result and then have your period arrive the following day. On the other hand, if you test early—even using one of those amazing baby-mind-reading tests that can detect hCG five days early—and it is negative, you may be setting yourself up for heartbreak of an entirely different kind. Though you may see a negative result, it might simply be because your levels are not high enough yet to show on the test.

My heart was broken. I had been so excited at the thought of being pregnant, and even better, I had worked out my possible due date, and it was two days before my birthday. I had been born two days before *my* mom's birthday, so I had already worked it all out in my head that I would have a girl and it would be a full-circle sort of deal. I had had this planned from the time I was fairly young. But, unfortunately, my period had come, a mere two days late. If I had not had the check-up, I would never have even known it was the start of a pregnancy.

# Joy for Another

Two weeks after the slightly late arrival of my period, I had a day off from work, and I was getting ready to go out with my mom. Just as I was about to leave, my phone rang. It was Chelsey calling, a strange occurrence in the middle of the afternoon on a weekday, but I didn't think much of it. I barely had a chance to say hello before my sister's voice came down the line.

"We have some news," Chelsey said.

"You're pregnant!" I said. Sure enough, she was. Eight weeks in, she and her husband had just come from their first ultrasound, where they had been able to catch a glimpse of their soon-to-be first child, their daughter Libby.

It is hard for me to properly express what I felt when I heard this news. I was absolutely, blissfully happy for my sister. All Chelsey had ever wanted in life was to be a wife and mother. Then, in a matter of a couple of years, and at 31 years old, she had it all. She and Ark had married the previous January, and now, after eight months of trying, she was pregnant. I was ecstatic for her. That might not have come through during our conversation, though, because I almost instantly started to bawl my eyes out. I was nearly inconsolable. On one hand, I truly was beyond happy for Chelsey, and on the other, I couldn't stop thinking: *Why her and not me?* Maybe not so much *Why her?* as *Why not both of us?*

In the interest of full disclosure, I will tell you that I was devastated. You see, Tosh and I had been together over three years before he proposed, over four before we were married, and we were fast approaching our fifth anniversary as a couple. I had waited patiently (or not so patiently, if you ask Tosh) for a marriage proposal that everyone had expected to come long before it had. Chelsey and Ark, on the other hand, had known each other for such a short time in comparison. They had begun dating two years before, in November, been engaged the October before their first anniversary, and married that January.

I cried when I found out about Chelsey's pregnancy because I was very sad for myself and Tosh. I cried because I wanted to experience pregnancy with my sister. I cried also because I felt very strong guilt over all of the above. I felt that I should be able to put myself and what had happened to me aside and just be happy for Chelsey.

Guilt is a difficult emotion to work through. The more I told myself that I should just be happy for Chelsey, the more I thought about how sad I was for myself. As a result, my guilt became deeper. Throughout Chelsey's pregnancy, and even after Libby was born, I found myself often mentally and emotionally removing myself from situations. During family dinners, when talk inevitably went to pregnancy, babies, and motherhood, I would shut down and tune it out. I couldn't ask everyone to stop talking about it. That would be selfish and just result in more guilt. I honed a true skill in tuning out when I couldn't handle the discussion. This is a skill that I still turn to today. Although I am much better and much more able to hear stories of pregnancy and motherhood, I still find myself escaping at times.

I will never get back that lost time when Chelsey was pregnant. I missed out on things, most often intentionally. It was, and still is, a choice I've had to make, in order to be able to be fully involved when I can handle it. That's the trick—knowing your own limitations. I had to find a way to be there for Chelsey as often as I could. If I wasn't there for her at all, how could I expect anyone to be there for me during my own pregnancy?

"Happy anniversary, honey! I peed on a stick and got you two pink lines for a present!" That is essentially how Tosh's and my fifth anniversary celebration started on February 2, 2011. I had started thinking that pregnancy was a possibility a few days before. I can honestly say that there were no indications, aside from the instinct that I had. About one week before, while visiting Chelsey, I had mentioned in passing that my mind didn't seem to be functioning normally.

"I was driving to work the other day," I can remember explaining to her. "I took the wrong turn to a house I've been driving to for two years."

"Maybe you're pregnant," Chelsey had piped up.

I didn't think it was possible. I'd had spotting that week, a normal occurrence for me in the week leading up to my period. Then, a couple of days before my period was due, the spotting had stopped, something which was *not* normal for my cycle. I still didn't think too much of it. I was still recovering from the disappointment of the previous month and was trying desperately not to get my hopes up.

Our anniversary was also the day that my period was due but didn't arrive. I enjoyed the romanticism of finding out we were pregnant on our anniversary, and more on a whim than a real instinct, I decided to do a pregnancy test.

What a whim that turned out to be! I went from ecstatic, terrified, and shocked, to instantly maternal—in a matter of seconds. There really is no adequate way of describing the feeling. You can only understand if you have been there yourself. It is the only time in my life that I've been equally scared and excited.

The planning started at dinner that night—what we would name it, how we would decorate the nursery, when its due date would be. After all, nobody ever thinks they'll be one of the unlucky ones who can't get pregnant, and once you do get pregnant, you certainly don't think you'll lose it. Sure, women have worries throughout pregnancy; I watched both of my sisters worry that it wouldn't go right. But deep down, you don't question that in nine months you'll be snuggling and making goo-goo noises at your newborn.

That night after dinner, we went straight home and told my mom our big news. By the end of the next day, everyone knew. Being a nanny at the time, I told my employers, so that they had as much time as possible to prepare. Our due date was October 13, 2011; I knew my employers would need time to sort out the details of their own child care.

I bought a pregnancy book and immediately started to watch what I ate. I began counting the glasses of water I drank in a day. I cut out coffee the morning after we found out. I was bound and determined to be the picture of health during my pregnancy.

The best part was that I was pregnant at the same time as Chelsey! We were about six weeks apart. I so anticipated pictures of our bumps facing each other and pictures of our babies lying side by side, while looking in awe at the difference in their size and knowing that, in time, it would no longer be noticeable.

On February 10, as I was lying in bed, my mom came into my room. Seeing immediately that she was upset about something, I sat straight up.

"Something's wrong with Chelsey," my mom managed to say.

At 11 weeks, Chelsey was having a bit of spotting. I gave my mom a healthy dose of "Everything is going to be fine" and "This is perfectly normal during pregnancy," and she seemed to feel a bit better.

"I know everything is going to be fine," my mom said to me that day. "You're both going to have beautiful babies, and everything is going to be fine."

Instantly, my guilt reared its ugly head again. On the inside I was panicking, thinking that Chelsey was going to miscarry. If she did, I would have to live with the guilt of being resentful of her pregnancy and ending up with a child of my own while watching her suffer a devastating loss. I worried about how difficult it would be for her to see me go through the stages of pregnancy while she was suffering the stages of grief.

By February 15, Chelsey was feeling much better, and I had my first sign of spotting. So began my first journey through miscarriage. I did my absolute best to ignore the spotting and convince myself it was a normal part of early pregnancy.

On the first day that I noticed it, I was visiting Courtney, and I mentioned it to her. "It's perfectly normal," she said. "I had spotting throughout the first 12 weeks with Mia, and everything was fine."

The brain is a funny thing. It's as though it has layers, like an onion. On one layer, I was thinking, *Everything is perfectly fine; spotting is completely normal*, while at the same time there was a different layer that was thinking, *I'm going to lose my baby*.

I talked to my sisters, my mom, and Tosh, looking for someone to reassure me. The funny thing is, even when people are doing everything they can to be reassuring, there's still that one layer of the onion telling you that reassurances don't mean squat.

On the second day of spotting, I called my doctor's office, and they also reassured me that it was fine. I spoke with women I knew who had experienced similar spotting and gone on to have perfectly healthy babies. I referred to my books on pregnancy and I scoured the Internet for information. Nothing made me feel better.

I was in pregnancy limbo. I couldn't become one of the women who lost their babies; it was a rare thing. It never happened. I didn't know anyone it had happened to. On the other hand—or another figurative layer of onion—I couldn't possibly be one of those women who got to have a normal, healthy pregnancy. I never had normal, healthy anything. I constantly suffered from digestion issues and chronic back pain. I suffered a bulging disc in my thoracic spine for absolutely no apparent reason. I'd never be someone to go through pregnancy *normally*.

It only requires a few pages, or even paragraphs, to describe a couple of days. In reality, two days felt like two lifetimes. The minutes felt as though they were ticking backward. I tried my absolute best to keep my sanity over the course of those two days. There are times in life, though, that sanity really just isn't an option. Everybody kept telling me to relax, that it was important I stay calm for the health of the baby. Oh, to be told to stay calm when your brain, and all of its many layers, is whirling out of control.

Once I hit the third day of light spotting, I couldn't take it anymore, and I called my doctor to book an appointment.

My doctor examined me and said everything looked fine. Because I hadn't even had my first official prenatal appointment yet, he decided to order some blood work and an ultrasound, as well. After the blood work was complete, Tosh and I went to have the ultrasound done. While I was apprehensive, I still believed deep down that it was all going to be okay. I was very much expecting to see, or at the very least hear, my baby that day.

I could tell something wasn't quite right when the ultrasound technician started asking questions about how far along I was and whether I'd had an ultrasound that showed the baby yet. When she asked my permission to do a vaginal ultrasound, I knew for sure something was up. I began to cry immediately and refused the vaginal ultrasound until I could speak to the doctor. It is impossible to describe the thoughts that went through my mind. I knew that something was wrong and that the tech didn't have the permission to give me any information.

Tosh was brought into the room to console me while we waited for the radiologist to tell us just what was going on.

"There is no indication of a fetus," the radiologist told us as he entered the room. "Either you were never pregnant, or you've already miscarried and it hasn't come out yet."

He followed this absolutely devastating (and coldly delivered) announcement by saying, "You have a retroverted uterus, so the baby may be hiding where we can't see it. Come back in a week, and we'll look again."

My heart split in two. Everyone has experienced at some point the crushing feeling of losing a loved one. It consumes you instantly; it doesn't hurt slowly. It punches you in the gut in an instant, leaving you numb and shocked all at the same time.

That is exactly how I felt when I heard this news. Except that this news didn't bring with it the finality that death brings. This news was that there was a possibility of death but the limited hope of life as well. I needed to know: *Was my baby okay, or was it already dead?*

I was still feeling sick from the changes to my hormones, still getting up to pee in the night, and still entirely mentally and emotionally attached to the baby that might or might not be growing inside me. I was one of those women who felt a connection to my baby the instant I knew it was in there. A small part of me thought I would be equally certain if it wasn't there anymore. But I wasn't certain at all, and I just had to wait.

The three days after the ultrasound were excruciating. My doctor's receptionist called with the results of my blood test, and they were as indecisive as everything else had been. My hCG levels were high but not as high as they would have liked, so—surprise, surprise—I would just have to wait and see what happened.

I was already completely exhausted from the days leading up to this. I had reached a point where I just wanted whatever was going to happen to happen. If I was destined to lose my baby, I just wanted it to be over and done with.

Along came the onion layers again. I wanted it to be over, whatever the outcome, but I desperately wanted the outcome to be that my baby was okay and still growing inside me. I tried to keep my hopes up, but with each passing moment, they were like a series of lit candles being blown out.

It was on the fourth day that I started to experience the cramping. It was extremely painful. I suffered contractions for four days and massive amounts of bleeding. The bleeding lasted just over two weeks. Add to this the negative effects of my pregnancy hormones plummeting back down to nothing, and the emotional distress of what I was losing, and you can believe that it was the worst four days of my life. I commented to Tosh one day that nobody seemed to realize how devastating it was to flush your baby down the toilet. I didn't miss work while I was experiencing this, and I was horrified at the idea that I was flushing my baby down some toilet! It sounds graphic and dramatic, but that is honestly what was going through my mind at the time.

Because discussing miscarriage is so taboo—which it absolutely should not be—it is something that most women will never even have a clue about. The body experiences physical contractions when it is going through a miscarriage. This, understandably, is more physically painful the further along you are in your pregnancy, but whether you are five weeks or twenty, your mind and heart already know that you are that baby's mother.

I can't even begin to imagine what it would be like to lose a baby further into pregnancy than the eight weeks I had reached. I don't necessarily believe the emotional pain would be worse; the loss isn't any bigger. The added physical pain, though, would be enough to make the emotional side of things that much harder to deal with. I try to remind myself as often as I can that, no matter how bad it was for me, it could always have been worse. It's a lesson that my parents ingrained into me: there is always someone out there who is going through something worse than you are. The thing is, while I try to remember this tidbit of wisdom, I can't help but feel that, if this is the worst thing I've ever experienced, does it really matter that people may be going through something more difficult? I feel for those people, I truly do, and I'm not so selfish as to think that my problems are as cumbersome as theirs, but they are most cumbersome to me.

# Everybody But Me

I can't remember a time in my life that was as difficult as this period. I know I've been very fortunate. I've had a very blessed life and have never really suffered great tragedy or heartache. It's true I was bullied in school, because I was so small and overwhelmingly shy, but I've always looked on that time and counted myself lucky that I experienced it. While it was excruciating to endure at the time, I truly believe I am better off because of it.

I hope that one day I'll look back on this experience and consider myself a stronger person because of it. The problem is that I'm tired of being strong. Courtney mentioned to me once that she would never have had the strength to endure what I've been through in the past year. I've had countless people tell me how strong I am and that I will be stronger than ever when I make it to the other side of this ordeal. The thing is, how strong does one person need to be? If I'm already as strong as everyone tells me I am, why do I need something to happen to me to make me even stronger? I have a really hard time reconciling this in my mind.

That's brings me to the other parental advice I've heard all my life: "Everything happens for a reason." This one is really hard for me to wrap my head around. What could the reason possibly be for a person going through this? And I don't just refer to myself. I'm talking about everyone who has been through something this difficult. That first miscarriage, even if it is the only one before you go on to have a healthy baby, will change the parenthood experience for the rest of your life. People who try for a year, or even a few months, and become frustrated with not getting pregnant forget this after they hold their beautiful baby in their arms.

My sister tried for eight months before she became pregnant. When she looks into Libby's eyes, how often do you think she thinks to herself, "If only it hadn't taken eight months"? On the other hand, every time *I* see a baby, think about a baby, see a pregnant woman, or hear that another woman is expecting, I think about what I lost. That is the key difference. Trying and not getting pregnant is not a loss. It is a struggle; I do not deny that, and it can be very difficult, but it is not a loss. There is no necessary grieving process attached to not getting pregnant right away.

In the months after my miscarriage, I was literally surrounded by pregnancy. My sister, Tosh's stepsister, Tosh's cousin, our neighbours—on both sides—our neighbour three doors down, and for the cherry on top, the psychiatrist that my doctor recommended I see. Yeah, that's right. The psychiatrist was eight months pregnant. As I walked into the doctor's office, I can clearly remember feeling a slight bit of hope. It was a marvellous feeling, one that I hadn't experienced in quite some time. I'm a strong believer in psychiatrists. I honestly believe that every single person should be required to go to one at least once in his or her life. Life scars us; we never get out alive. So I waltzed into the office that day feeling good about things, and then . . . I saw it . . . The psychiatrist looked as though she could go into labour right there in the room. And just like that, my recently slightly inflated balloon burst,

"So, Lindsey, what are you here for today?" the psychiatrist asked me as I took a seat.

I quickly replied with, "I've had two miscarriages, and I don't think I'll be able to talk to you about it."

To her credit, she openly said she couldn't blame me and offered to end the appointment right then and there. I figured I was already there, so I might as well give it a shot. I made it through a 50-minute appointment, and I never saw that psychiatrist again.

It certainly didn't end there, though. Everywhere I went, women were pregnant. I couldn't escape it. We'd go to Dairy Queen for a treat, and as I stood there waiting, I would be sandwiched smack in between two very pregnant girls. I started a new part-time job, and the girl I was going to be working with was pregnant. Family members were getting pregnant left, right, and centre. One of Tosh's best friends had met Tosh's stepsister at our wedding, and they'd started dating. They were pregnant.

Courtney was a tremendous help at this point. Having already had her children, Courtney was one person that I could easily be around. Courtney understood not to talk about pregnancy and babies and, because of the age or her own children, she didn't need to. Owen and Mia were five and three and, because I'd already spent years loving and adoring them, I was fine to continue to be with them.

I had to escape the constant pregnancies in some way, and it seemed that the only thing to do was to take a much-needed break—from thinking about and trying for babies, from people, and from life in general.

# A Second Chance

In an attempt to deal with the sorrow that I admittedly was not dealing with very well, Tosh and I planned a trip. It was not just any trip. We ended up going to Europe for almost three weeks. We consciously planned this trip so that it would include the day that our baby would have been born, October 13. To say the very least, those were 17 of the best days I've ever had. It was phenomenal. We started off with three days in London, almost two weeks travelling around Italy, and then it was back to London for a few more days.

We were relaxed and happy. We were back to our regular selves. We just enjoyed each other's company and relished how fortunate we were to be able to take such a huge trip. We spent the entire time with my cousin Erin, who was living in London, and

I had a blast with her. I had lived with Erin; her brother, Devon; and my aunt and uncle years before, and I absolutely adored Erin.

We took in all the history and the tourist sites. We wandered the streets of cities that were hundreds of years older than Canada. We tried to live the culture and, oh boy, did we eat the food.

I had a moment on October 13, thinking about where I'd thought I'd be (at home, a brand-new mom) and where I was (Stintino, Italy). The two were so completely different from one another; it was like another world. I was sad that day. I would have much rather been in Calgary, giving birth, having just given birth, or waiting to give birth. I did pretty well, though. I had a good cry, a glass (or bottle—or two!) of wine, and enjoyed my holiday.

A few days after we returned home from Europe, we were thrilled to find out that we were pregnant. We had conceived on the trip.

This was going to be it! Everything that had happened so far had happened so that this would be our first child. I'm one who puts a lot of stock into dates and is always searching for hidden meaning in everything, so I was ecstatic that our child's story had started during such a memorable time in our lives.

I went to my doctor the day after we saw the positive result, and everything looked good. I was due July 3, but being the ridiculously proud Canadian that I am, I was determined to have it on the first, Canada Day.

As I had the first time, I told my family right away. This was partly because I was so certain this one would work but also because I wanted them there with me through the entire journey. And the small voice in the back of my mind told me that it was important for them to know, just in case anything happened, and I needed them to support me through it.

Everyone was over the moon. We all believed that this was the explanation for why we had suffered before. It was so that we could truly appreciate this baby and how blessed we were. My sister wanted us to have a boy, as she thought Roman would be a perfect name for a little guy conceived in Italy! We were all so excited. Chelsey gave me a Jewish "eye" to wear around my wrist to protect me. The eye is a small bead that you put on a piece of string or ribbon and wear as a bracelet. The idea behind it is that if someone thinks mean or harmful thoughts about you, the eye will keep them from harming you. I put the bead on a piece of ribbon and tied it around my wrist right away. If the ribbon comes undone and the eye falls off, the belief is that it was protecting you from something and you are not to put it back on.

This time, when I started to suspect a problem, I didn't tell anyone. I didn't want to believe that it could be happening again. It was a mere five days after we found out we were pregnant that I started feeling the cramps. I did everything I could to convince myself that it was the little tyke nestling in there, getting nice and cozy for the next few months. I took another pregnancy test to ease my mind. Unfortunately, the second line on this test was very faint, which had the effect of worrying me even more. Why was the line fainter than it had been five days earlier? What was wrong with my baby?

I jumped into the shower to try to make myself relax. It was in the shower, while I was soaping up, that the piece of ribbon holding my "eye" onto my wrist came unknotted. I didn't even turn the shower off. I jumped out, grabbed the phone, and dialled Chelsey as quickly as I could. Dripping wet, with the cordless phone cradled between my ear and shoulder, and holding the bracelet in place on my wrist, I told Chelsey exactly what had happened. My eye hadn't fallen off; the knot had come undone, but I had caught it before it came all the way off. This was a technicality that Chelsey wasn't equipped to answer. So I sat on the edge of the tub and waited for her to call back with an answer from Ark. If the eye had technically fallen off, I couldn't put it back on as that would be bad luck. But if it hadn't fallen off, I couldn't take it off, or that would ruin its purpose and be bad luck as well.

Chelsey called back about 15 minutes later, though it seemed like a lot longer than that. She told me I couldn't wear the eye anymore. I put it in the garbage and actually felt a bit of solace in the idea that it had protected me.

The bleeding started later that night. It wasn't as bad this time, as I wasn't as far along. But it was equally painful, if not more so. I think I was numb at this point—dazed and shocked. The doctors had told me that the odds of having two miscarriages were so slim that I honestly hadn't given much thought to it. Of course, it had always been in the back of my mind. Even if you are a woman who has never had one, I don't think anyone can go through a pregnancy without thinking about the possibility.

I certainly wasn't the only one stunned. It was as if the air had been let out of everyone's lungs. We were all sad, confused, and angry—very angry. The first thing that went through my mind, and I think the minds of most of the people involved, was that something must be wrong with me. The chemical pregnancy had been pretty much forgotten after the first miscarriage. One miscarriage was a fluke, but two consecutively must mean something bad.

# Lessons Learned

A lot of people have said things to me that, although they didn't realize it or mean it, were inappropriate. When people tell you that you just need to relax or that it will happen when you least expect it, they don't realize that while that line makes sense to women who can't get pregnant (but is likely equally as annoying and anger-inducing), it is an absolutely awful thing to say to a woman who continuously miscarries. It's essentially saying that you are entirely at fault for your miscarriages and that if you could just relax, your baby would survive.

Our pregnancy in October had started while we were vacationing in a small Italian villa on the island of Sardinia. We had been relaxed. We hadn't even known we were pregnant until a few days after we got home, and then—*bam*—I miscarried within five days. Not exactly enough time to get so worked up and stressed out that my body somehow killed the baby that was trying to develop inside it. When people speak before they think and make such a comment, I smile, nod, and say something like, "Whatever is meant to happen will happen." Of course, what I'm really thinking is that people just don't understand. For a long time I thought that it was selective ignorance, that people were choosing not to hear what I was telling them and, as a result, not providing the most effective reassurances. It took me a long time to realize that, in most cases, people were just saying the only thing they knew to say. It is similar to when a death occurs or a divorce; it is difficult to know what to say, so people usually just end up using a generic line. I've learned over time that people think it will help if they offer advice—even the completely wrong advice!

After my latest miscarriage, I had a few people ask me if I was "frustrated" by what was happening. To anyone reading this who is looking for ways to support a friend or loved one through a miscarriage, I say, "Don't—I repeat, *do not*—ask them if they're frustrated!" Frustration is when you record your favourite TV show and the recording stops with seconds left at the end of the program. Frustration is when there's an accident on your way to work and you end up late. Failed pregnancies are not frustrating—they are heartbreaking. In my case, my miscarriages were early enough that I was still coming down from the high of discovering I was pregnant when I hit the horrible low of realizing I was losing it. Frustration is not an emotion that I think I felt at any point. I was frustrated for the first few months of trying to get pregnant. I didn't think there could be anything more difficult than trying and failing month after month.

I've had people tell me that it is just as painful and heartbreaking to try for a few months to get pregnant without success as it is to lose a baby to miscarriage. I can tell you that it isn't. I know perfectly well what it is like to be disappointed month after month when your period arrives. I also know that I would give just about anything to go back to that time when we were trying and not getting pregnant. I would rather try for years than go through even one miscarriage.

I'll never forget the time that, as I learned that yet another woman in my life was expecting, she told me that she felt bad for me but she had to be happy for herself. She said a few times, "I deserve it," or "I deserve to be a mom." This absolutely broke my heart. Saying that to someone who has suffered multiple miscarriages is as good as saying they deserve the heartache they are experiencing.

Having children isn't about deserving them or not deserving them. There are women who deserve children who can't have them. Having children or going through what I've been through isn't about deserving it or not; it is about being the kind of person who can grow from experiences. And maybe, just a little bit, it's about being a protector of others, so they don't have to face the same fate.

I've racked my brain trying to figure out how I can show some women that what they say is inappropriate and completely out of context. I've experienced sleepless nights trying to find a way to make them understand just how hurtful their comments are. It took me a long to time to realize that it wasn't them who had to change; it was me. Rather than trying to teach other people what I thought to be important lessons, I began to look for the lessons that I could learn.

I learned that it is up to us to decide what we take from life, what we choose to hear in what others say. No doubt there are times when people are genuinely trying to be mean or hurtful. Those people can't be changed, and at the end of the day, it is usually because of an issue that they have with themselves, not with the people they are mean to. For the most part, I've learned to believe that it isn't human nature to be mean. It is in our nature to be kind, to say nice things, to encourage, and to inspire. I've learned to take something that might be seen as inappropriate or uncaring as an honest attempt to say the right thing when not knowing what the right thing is.

So, I guess my advice would be twofold. First, don't put any stock into what others say to you. They are trying, in the only way they know how, to help. And as for those who aren't even trying, who just really don't appreciate how difficult it is, there may come a time when you need to remove those people from your life. Even if it's only for a short time, there is no reason why you should have to put up with a lack of support from anyone during such a difficult time.

I've had to cut ties with a few people. I've deleted people from my Facebook and stopped talking to friends. And I've realized through all of this that my real friends are the ones who say, "We'll be right here when you're ready." They don't hate me for not being strong enough or begrudge that I'm not there during their exciting time. They patiently wait for me to be okay.

My sister is a great example of this. I had a really hard time with her pregnancy, but she never pushed it on me. She never made me feel bad if I couldn't bring myself to ask her how she was doing. Hell, the day she went into labour she was more worried about how I was doing in the waiting room alone with my thoughts. There she was, giving birth five weeks early, and her concern was for me. Now, that is a true friend.

Every once in a while you feel the amazing love of people and realize just how much others care. Tosh's Auntie Shelly sent me an email right in the middle of the pain; it was entitled *For All Mothers (Including Soon-to-Be Mothers).* The email was a tale of a woman asking her mom if she should have children. The woman's mom went on to describe what an amazing journey it is to have a child and how it would change her life. The story isn't the point, though. The point is that Shelly saw me as a mom-to-be. I don't have to be pregnant or have a baby bump; I am an expectant mother, just like all the pregnant women out there.

Always remember that there is someone out there who has gone or is going through more than you are. Feel what you are feeling. For me personally, this is the hardest thing I've ever had to go through. I don't know pain worse than what I've felt in the last year, but I also know that there *is* worse and that, despite everything, I'm fortunate that my situation isn't any worse than it is.

Having said that, it doesn't hurt any less when people try to diminish what you are experiencing. You can tell yourself that things could be worse until you are blue in the face, but at the end of the day, if it is the worst thing you've been through, it doesn't really matter how much worse it could be. If you feel awful, you feel awful. You can't always tell yourself you could feel worse, because you've never experienced worse, so you can't understand what that feels like, anyway. That is why you hear people say "I can't imagine what you're going through." You shouldn't feel bad for not understanding or caring about what others are going through. Feel your pain as much as you want.

Again, the people who understand this, who love you unconditionally, will be there for you when you come out of it. Whether you've kept them close or at arm's length, true loved ones won't hold it against you.

# Answers

After the third miscarriage, we were welcomed to the Early Pregnancy Loss Clinic. Our first fertility appointment was a bit of a letdown. When we'd found out we had an appointment, I had been so excited. I'd thought, *Okay, here we go. Everything is going to be fixed now.* When the appointment day arrived, it was one catastrophe after another. First of all, the clinic had put our appointment time in their system as being at 9:00 o'clock. The package they sent out to us, however, said 10:00. So, when I arrived at 9:55 and was told the doctor had a 10:00 and "he might be able to see you today," I was ready to jump the desk and demand my appointment then and there. To make matters worse, Tosh (not surprisingly) arrived at the appointment 15 minutes late. It is a very depressing experience to be sitting alone in the waiting room of a fertility clinic with nothing but couples surrounding you. Luckily for

Tosh, he walked into the office door as the nurse walked out from the back and called our names.

Now, in the weeks leading up to the appointment we had received a package in the mail, with questionnaires asking every single detail of our histories, both pre-and post-miscarriage. I happily completed every single question, thinking it was great that they were going to get to know us before we saw the doctor. That way it wouldn't be a waste of time. This isn't exactly how it went down. The doctor came in, asked us a few of the questions that we had already answered on the questionnaire, told us about the standard tests we would have to have done, and then . . . left. But, wait! Where were my answers? And how did he know I would need the standard tests, like everyone else? Surely our situation was unique. The whole thing was so routine, as if it didn't matter to him who we were or what our history was. We were just like every other couple he'd ever seen.

I understand that this is the way things are done. They can't have answers for every single couple the first time they walk through the door. The tests they were going to run were definitely standard, but they should also provide answers. I just needed to be patient. The problem was that I was done with being patient at this point. I'd lost three babies, and I wanted someone to tell me why and where to go from here. It was at this time that I realized I didn't even care what the answer was going to be—I just wanted an answer.

I've been asked a number of times if I'm sad when thinking about the possibility that I may never have children naturally. I've thought about the various answers many times, and I've concluded that I'm not sad about that aspect of our journey. I'm not concerned with *how* we end up having children. I know that we *will* be parents, whether they be biological children or adopted, carried by myself or someone else. It will happen one way or the other. What I am sad about is what we've already been through.

I know other women who have suffered miscarriages, and they all say that when you do end up with a baby, it's as if the miscarriages were meant to be, so that you would have that exact baby. These women have also all gone on to carry their babies to term and given birth themselves.

Tosh and I have made the decision together that we will not be going through fertility treatments in an attempt to have biological children. We are going to adopt. We are absolutely ecstatic about this and truly believe that it is the right thing for us. Even though we have consciously made this decision, it doesn't take away from the hurt that we've experienced or my sadness that I will never carry a child. I can't go through another loss; I won't survive it. I look at some women who go to the ends of the earth to carry children in their wombs. They will endure anything and everything for that experience to be their own. Each couple needs to make that decision for themselves, in their own best interest.

While Tosh and I are excited about our road to parenthood, our journey will never be an entirely happy one. It will always be slightly tainted by what we have been through. That doesn't mean we won't be overjoyed when we do end up with a child. In fact, we may be even happier *because* of the pain we've suffered. The pain will never go away, though. For the rest of our lives, the loss and suffering will be a part of our journey to becoming parents, and that is what makes me sad.

# Mixed Emotions

I went through a period when it was very difficult for me to be out in groups. This happened mostly in groups of women who either had children or were pregnant. For the most part, the women understood the difficulty I faced. It wasn't entirely selfish on my part, either. Women go out together to talk about their lives and to vent. When it is a group of women who also happen to be mothers, kids come up in the conversation. I knew that mostly everyone would try to be respectful of me and not discuss their kids too much.

How is that fair, though? Why should my difficulties affect their time together? I don't ever want to take away from anybody else, which is why I consciously decide to skip things sometimes.

There are relationships that I had to put on hold, pregnant girlfriends who I just couldn't be as close with as I had been. I even had to step away from Chelsey a bit. That was painful. I didn't go to the family lunch where she announced her pregnancy. It was hard—I wanted to be there, but I physically, mentally, and emotionally couldn't do it.

I've declined invitations to baby showers and passed up the opportunity to go to parties where I know pregnancies are going to be announced.

I've done this for selfish reasons, because it was physically, emotionally, and mentally too much for me. I've also done it for the sake of the people who are announcing their pregnancies or celebrating the birth of their child. I've done it because I don't want someone else's joy to be interrupted by anyone thinking about my pain. Again, I've explained this to friends, and while some understand completely, others only see the selfish side of what I'm doing.

It is painful for me to picture people with their children. Sometimes I think about my sister rocking Libby in her bedroom and having sweet, loving moments. This is very difficult for me. Sometimes I can hear our neighbours' babies crying, and it physically hurts, because I don't have that. When parents complain about the not-so-wonderful parts of parenting, it makes me sad, because I would give anything to experience the bad so I could experience the good too. I'm happy that these people have what they do, but I want it, too. I don't see the rhyme or reason in me not being able to have it. And it is hard to find out that others are pregnant. With computers and social networking, it is especially difficult, because the news is everywhere.

Women post their happy news, pictures of their ever-growing bumps, and even the positive pregnancy tests. I recently decided to stop going on Facebook after yet another happy announcement.

This particular announcement did it for me, because the friend was due in October, which is when my baby would have been one year old.

There are plenty of mixed emotions that arise, and they all seem to surface at the same time. The only solace I've been able to take from others' happy news is that they try so hard to understand how difficult it is for me. Not everyone does, of course, but pretty much all my friends and family who are expecting or have recently had children at least make the effort.

# Low Point

I reached an extremely low point about three months after the last miscarriage and right around the first anniversary of the first miscarriage. It was right around the time that we were starting tests at the fertility clinic, and for the first time, despite all of the well-wishers and positivity coming to us, things weren't looking very promising.

I was suffering from a great deal of pain, something which I've always had, but my state of absolute depression was making the pain that much worse—and I'm sure the pain was making the depression worse, as well.

I was really beginning to shut people out, not because they weren't helping but because I had reached a point where I wasn't sure I wanted the help anymore. I wanted to be miserable, and yes, in honour of this tale being completely candid, I wanted it all to end. I wanted to end my life. *Whew*, that's a hard thing to say.

I want to make absolutely sure, before I continue with this part of my story, that my family knows these desires had nothing to do with them or a lack of support or help from them. I've never fully understood what a mind can be experiencing when it is contemplating suicide. I've always wondered why suicidal people didn't think they had anyone to talk to or anyone who loved them. I can honestly say now that, when you reach that point, it doesn't matter if the entire world has your back. When you want pain to end, sometimes you think that death is the only way to make it happen.

I would sit in the bathtub at night, thinking about how I was going to go about it. I considered slitting my wrists, but being someone who is terrified of needles, I didn't think that was the right option. I thought about driving my car into a median and making it look like an accident, but then I thought, *What if I accidently cause an accident and hurt someone else in my attempt to end my own pain?*

I eventually settled on pills as being the best method, but then I read that people who take pills are more often than not asking for help, and they don't really intend to die as much as bring attention to what they are going through. I wanted there to be absolutely no mistake that I'd wanted to die. So I landed back at slitting my wrists. It would only take a second, after all, to do the actual cutting, and it wouldn't be a horrible way for Tosh to find me.

I even reached a point when I decided what day I would do it. February 18, 2012 was going to be the day I would kill myself and end the misery that I was feeling. Why this date? Well, for starters, it was one year to the day that I had suffered the first miscarriage. I found it strangely poetic that my life would end on the anniversary of the day my baby's life had ended. It was perfect: Tosh was at a party, so I had the house to myself. He was having fun with his family and friends, so he would always be able to remember that the day I died had also been a good day, at the start, at least.

As Tosh went to his party that night, I was an absolute wreck. I can honestly look back on it and say it was the worst night of my life. I began thinking about my sisters, at home with their kids. I also thought about Tosh, at the party he was attending, where a great number of the people he was with had babies, toddlers, and children—either that or they were expecting.

I hated my life in that moment. I hated what had happened; I hated what was still happening. I hated almost every other woman who had children at home or children on the way. I hated that I felt like less of a woman because I couldn't do what seemed to come so easily to everyone else. I hated that I felt I was letting Tosh down.

Even with all of those horrible thoughts and feelings, the one thought that I hated most was what I would be doing to my family if I followed through on my plan. I *couldn't* bring myself to let Tosh suffer with the pain of finding me when he got home. I couldn't imagine what my nieces and nephew would think of me as they grew up and were told stories about me. I couldn't bear to think of my mom, dad, and sisters always wondering whether there was something they could have done.

I can clearly remember sitting in the tub that night, ready to do the unthinkable, and suddenly realizing that I just couldn't. Maybe that means that I was never really going to do it. I don't know. All I know is that my family saved me that night, and they didn't even know that I needed saving.

I put suicide to the back of my mind, for a while, anyway. It was only about three weeks after that when I started thinking about it again. I was being invited to baby showers that I didn't have the strength to attend and family dinners where I couldn't face talking about someone else's pregnancy. Once again, I planned the night that I was going to do it. Tosh was going to the family dinner that I just couldn't face, and the baby shower that I didn't have the strength for was at the same time. It was perfect. I'd tell each party I couldn't go because I would be with the other. In reality, I would stay home and do what I hadn't been able to a few weeks ago.

Again, when it came down to it, I couldn't do it. I couldn't imagine leaving my family feeling any sense of responsibility for my suicide. I couldn't leave Tosh wondering where it had all gone wrong and never really having the answers. And, I realized, I had to fight. I wanted a life with Tosh, a good one. As good as the one we'd thought we were going to have—only different.

I have to say this now, because if it stops even one person who reads this book from doing what I wanted to do, it is worth saying. If you, at any point, start to feel like you can't go on, *get help*! It doesn't have to be professional help. It can be a family member, a friend, a colleague—anyone who you feel you can talk to.

I turned to Chelsey. I knew she had experience with depression, and I knew she would not only handle it with a level head but she would also be able to appreciate what I was feeling.

I still feel bad that she was the one I turned to. There she was, with a brand-new baby, the happiest time in her life, and her little sister was calling her, saying she wanted to kill herself. It was selfish of me, and I will always feel bad about that.

She did help, though. She helped as no one else could at the time. Being on maternity leave, she was able to call me or take my calls at any time. Being a nurse, she knew what I needed to do from a medical perspective. Being my big sister, she knew what to say to me to calm me down and ease my mind. She saved me. She convinced me to go on antidepressants, and she put me in contact with a psychiatrist who she thought could help.

Not everyone is fortunate enough to have the kind of support I've experienced. I've said it already, but I want to say it again: it really is wrong that miscarriage isn't a more talked-about subject. There are groups out there that can help. There are other women who have been through, or are in the middle of, similar situations. There are psychiatrists and counsellors who specialize in pregnancy loss. Find these people. Find the people who can help you through the pain. If there isn't a group in your area or you aren't comfortable joining an existing group, start your own. You can even find groups online, which can be a great option, because there is anonymity to them.

I got help. I started taking the pills, seeing a therapist, and talking more openly with people about what I was feeling. I very slowly started to get back into exercising, which helped a ton. I threw myself into my new job and realized that, without intention, I'd stumbled into a career that I loved, working with people who were becoming my friends.

# A Visitor

A few months after we found out that we wouldn't be able to have biological children naturally, I had a lovely dream, in which my dearly missed grandpa visited me. My grandpa has been gone for six years, and I do dream about him from time to time, but this dream was a very special one. I love dreaming about my grandpa. I really do believe that it is his way of coming back, if only for a short time, and letting me know he is doing all right.

In my dream, I was riding my bike to work, enjoying the nice weather and listening to the music through my headphones. Suddenly, I felt a gentle tapping on my shoulder. I was aware that it was a person tapping my shoulder with a finger. *But*, I wondered, *how is that even possible? If I'm on my bike, who could possibly be tapping my shoulder?* I turned my head, and lo and behold, there was my grandpa!

I pulled my headphones out of my ears, and in a voice crossed with absolute shock and joy, I said, "Hey, Grandpa, long time no see." To this my wonderful grandpa replied, "Hi. Sorry I haven't been around for a while. Just wanted to check in and catch up. Do you have time for a coffee?" Well, as you can imagine, when your deceased grandpa asks you to join him for coffee, you certainly don't tell him you have to get to work!

After a few minutes of idle chit-chat, Grandpa changed the topic of conversation, saying to me, "I have something I need to tell you, and I'm telling you because I know you will pass it on to your sisters." I can clearly remember in the dream feeling as though I was about to hear bad news, something that none of us would want to hear but had to, so we could prepare for whatever was to come. This was not the case at all.

"Owen, Mia, and Libby are the three most beautiful children ever," continued my grandpa. "They are amazing, and they will do amazing things. And I know you can't see it yet, but I want you to know that *I* have seen it, and you have something amazing coming to you. You just have to be patient and wait for it." And with that, one of my favourite men in the world said, "I have to go now," and he was gone.

I woke up startled and in tears. I had a real sense that my grandpa had been there (as I always do after these dreams). I had such a sense of peace and even excitement about the wonderful mystery that was in store for me. I was also a bit annoyed because, being who I am, I didn't want to be patient and wait to find out what it was!

I immediately called my mom and sisters to tell them about the experience. They, of course, wanted me to call and tell my grandma about it as well. So I phoned my grandma, but the line was busy. About 15 minutes after I'd tried to get her, my own phone rang, and spookily enough, it was my grandma. Now, for a bit of background, Gram and I don't talk very often. Not for a lack of wanting to—it is honestly because I am so damn busy. If you don't know how to text, I don't have a lot of opportunity to call you. Gram never calls my house, because she knows I'm never home. I'd venture to guess that she calls maybe once in six months or so. So for her to call when I was trying to get hold of her was a bit strange, to say the least.

It got weirder. She told me that she had tried me about 15 minutes earlier, but my line had been busy. We figured out that we had been trying to call each other at the same time. As if that wasn't enough, she said, "I was just sitting here and thinking about you and thought I would get lucky and catch you before you left for work." She couldn't explain why she'd had the urge to call, but I was able to explain it for her. Grandpa had told her to call me. I told her all about the dream, and she, like everyone else, was stunned.

I really started thinking about this dream and what it meant. I understood that Grandpa was trying to tell me that I would have my time to become a mother and that, when it did finally happen, it would be more amazing than I could imagine. But, as has been the case so many times over the past year and a bit, I couldn't reconcile for myself why it had to be me. Why was *I* the one who had to wait for something wonderful? And, more importantly, why was I the one who had to go through such heartache to get to that wonderful point?

I started to think that maybe there really was a reason behind it all. I've said it before, but I'll say it again. I wouldn't wish on my worst enemy the pain that I have experienced. Yes, it is very difficult for me to see other women pregnant and becoming and being moms, but I would never wish for someone not to have that joy and miracle. It's just that *I* want it too. So I started thinking that maybe I was the one going through this because I understood that. Maybe my Grandpa knew that either I or one of my sisters would have to experience this, and he knew I was the one who could handle it, learn from it, and become stronger as a result. Maybe I was a protector for my sisters. By going through this myself, I saved one of them the heartache of going through it.

That was when my perspective really started to change. I wasn't going through this because I was deserving of something bad. I was going through it because I had the ability to get through it.

I think it was after this dream that things really started to turn around for me. I started believing that, while it had been an awful experience, one that would live with me forever, there was a purpose to it. Maybe there was more than one purpose. Maybe it was partially to protect my sisters. Possibly it had happened so that Tosh and I would be led to adopt a child that had been born into the world for us to raise. Maybe it was because my wonderful grandpa had passed away just days before he would have found out about his first great-grandchild, and he deserved to have great-grandchildren with him.

Whatever the reason or reasons, I was coming to terms with it—finally. I started noticing that it wasn't quite so hard for me to see pregnant women. I started reaching out to the friends that I hadn't had much contact with over the course of their own pregnancies. Some of these friends welcomed me back with open arms. This, I believe, is a true testament to what amazing women these friends are. Some still haven't welcomed me back, not truly, anyway. Some likely never will.

It became less painful to see adorable babies and learn of women who were expecting. I don't know if the pain will ever completely go away, and I certainly still have days when I don't handle it as well, but for the most part, I was feeling pretty good about life.

I wasn't talking about my babies, miscarriage, pain, and anguish nearly as much either. I realized that for a time I had been completely consumed by it and it had come up in nearly every conversation. Then, one day it seemed as though this just stopped. When I would meet friends for coffee, I wouldn't feel the need to discuss it anymore.

My friends and family, being the intuitive wonders that they are, must have noticed this as well. They didn't ask quite so often. Not because they didn't care anymore, but because they noticed that my wounds were healing, and they didn't want to pull off the scabs.

I started seeking motivation and signs in everyday life. I read books about people who had experienced connections with the "other side." This did wonders for me. Knowing that people truly believed there was another side led me to believe that my babies were out there, somewhere. I absolutely believe, with the strongest conviction possible, that my babies had souls. They didn't survive long inside of me, but they did exist, and they still do. Their souls are out there.

Tosh and I each got tattoos, which include different segments of the poem I wrote for our babies. This is something that will live in us (and quite literally *on* us) for the rest of lives.

I started seeking out quotes and sayings that I was able to find meaning and strength in. One quote in particular that really stuck with me was spoken by Rose Kennedy: "It has been said, 'time heals all wounds.' I do not agree. The wounds remain. In time, the mind, protecting its sanity, covers them with scar tissue and the pain lessens. But it is never gone."

This quote meant a lot for me. I was trying to heal, to move on with my life. But at the same time, I was desperate to ensure that healing didn't go hand in hand with forgetting. This quote helped me to realize that, while I healed for the sake of my own survival, it didn't necessarily mean that I was forgetting.

The babies would always be a part of me, and I could never forget them. I did need to move forward, though. It was time to be a wife, daughter, sister, and friend to those I loved—and, eventually, to be a mom to the miracle that would become mine.

# A Loss of a Different Kind

As Christmas 2012 approached, it was, as the Christmas before, difficult for me. It is hard not to think about which Christmas this would have been for my children. Two of them would have been celebrating their second Christmas. For the third, it would have been the first Christmas.

I often wonder when these times will get easier. When will I stop thinking about those days?—their first Christmas, the day I found out I was expecting, their due dates, the days I knew I had lost a baby. I don't know if those feelings of loss will ever go away. As I've already said, I don't really want them to. I'd perhaps like them to become fewer and farther between, but I don't really want them gone entirely.

This year Christmas was horrendous, and it had nothing to do with my own memories and thoughts.

Chelsey, who was 16 weeks pregnant by December 2012, started having mild cramps one week before Christmas. After a couple of days, she decided to go to the emergency room, where they performed an ultrasound that indicated everything with the baby was fine. A couple more days passed, and because the cramping hadn't subsided, she went to see her obstetrician. Again she was told that the baby seemed healthy and that her cervix was shut nice and tight. She was having contractions, but they could very well pass.

I was optimistic. After all, my grandpa had basically told me that I was the one to suffer so that my sisters would be protected. In my wildest nightmares, I never believed that two of us could be put through such tremendous pain.

On Christmas, Chelsey started feeling better. The contractions weren't as bad. Did we have a Christmas miracle happening?

By the evening the contractions were back and worse than ever. Around nine o'clock that night, her water broke. Not long after that, she felt some discomfort in her back and some pressure in her belly. Her instinct was to push. Chelsey and Ark's son was born and passed away on December 25, 2012.

*Are you kidding me!* I thought. What the hell was the purpose of this? Why did Chelsey have to endure something so horrendous and painful?

I was beyond angry; I was furious that it had happened and furious that I hadn't been able to protect her, which I had come to believe was my role. The pain, for our entire family, was too much! And I knew all too well that the true pain for Chelsey hadn't even begun.

I wanted to put her in a bubble and save her from everything she would experience. I wanted to shut the world out for her until the pain, anger, sadness, and feeling of betrayal lessened.

It killed me that I couldn't do this for my sister. I knew that she had to go through the emotions—the grief, the pain, all of it. All I could do was be there for her.

Chelsey and I developed a unique understanding of one another. In all honesty, it's one I wish we didn't have, given the circumstances that led to it, but one that I appreciate nonetheless.

Chelsey suddenly understood everything I had felt for the past two years. I suddenly understood being the person who wanted to make everything better for someone that I loved more than words could express. We became protectors of each other. It wasn't solely *my* role anymore; it was one that we shared.

I do have to say that, in the little time since Chelsey lost her baby boy, she has amazed me. She is far stronger than I ever imagined her to be or gave her credit for. I've always admired Chelsey, but my admiration has grown now.

# An Open Letter

To everyone who has been a part of this journey, I want to thank you. Whether you were one of the wonderful people who were there to support me every step of the way or you were one of the people who ultimately showed your true colours and let me down, I still thank you. If it wasn't for the latter select few, I wouldn't appreciate just how amazing the good ones are.

For everyone who thought I should have been stronger and able to handle other people's joy above my pain, I pray for you that you are never faced with anything as difficult as this. I do sincerely apologize for not being able to share in your joy. Unfortunately, there are times in our lives that we aren't in control of how we deal with things. Just as unfortunately, the difficult times often leave us unable to appreciate the happy times for others. I do not begrudge you your happiness. If I ever left you with that impression, I am sincerely sorry for that. I do begrudge how some people expected me to act a certain way and refused to even attempt to understand. And I begrudge certain peoples' thinking that my pain and inability to be there for them all of the time was the result of personal ill will toward them. It was never about anyone else. It was purely, selfishly, about me.

Now, back to those whom I remain in awe of to this day, for the support and love they lavished on me and on Tosh. It's true what you hear about times of peril and sadness: if you look hard enough, you can always find some good in every situation. I realize now that the good I can take from all of this is the knowledge that my relationships with certain people are stronger than ever. In fact, I have relationships with people that I wasn't even moderately close to before any of this. I've discovered true friends and lasting friendships during this time. I know that these people will always be there for me, through anything, because they came to me during such a difficult time. And I truly hope that there will be a time when the others can start to realize what I've been through and maybe come around a bit.

I also want to thank some of the people who made comments that they didn't think about before they spoke. One of these was the friend who announced her pregnancy to me and told me that, while she felt awful for me, *she* deserved to be pregnant. True. Absolutely true. Everyone deserves that, if that is what they want. I held on to that comment for a very long time, because to me, it was saying that I deserved what I had gotten: the pain, misery, and heartache. It said that, while she deserved a child, for some reason I didn't, or I would have one. I realized nearly a year after this comment was made that I had the choice to take it in an entirely different context. I did not deserve the losses that I'd suffered, and

I absolutely did not deserve to be deprived of being a biological mother. I *do* deserve to save a child, though, and raise it with all of the love, compassion, and joy that Tosh and I can offer. I had to go through heartache to get to it, but I am absolutely deserving of the love of the child that I will be fortunate enough to receive one day.

My mom, dad, and beautiful sisters have always been my everything. I am so amazingly lucky to have been born to the two most wonderful parents in the world and even luckier to have ended up with my favourite two women as sisters. Each of them got me through the past two years in his or her own way. They are all responsible for saving me.

When Tosh came into my life, he instantly became my new everything. He was a natural extension of my family and the people I held closest to my heart. Tosh helped me to survive the past two years, and he is the person whom I survived for.

My marriage to Tosh was tested very early on. I had days when I didn't think we would be able to get through it. When I didn't feel supported, when I truly believed that he didn't care as much about our lost babies, I didn't see how our marriage could possibly survive. I was wrong. He did care and still does. He mourned them too, just in a different way.

Tosh and I have found strength in each other that we hadn't known was there—until we needed it. This is partly because of those who have supported us, and it is partly because of how we've supported each other.

Tosh and I have so much to look forward to. It's certainly not the life we'd thought we were in for, but what a life it will be! We've already experienced so many wonderful things together and created countless wonderful memories. I'm excited to see what the future has in store for us.

Finally, I want to say this to my perfect three babies, who will never know this world and whom, unfortunately, this world will never know: To me, you are perfection. I loved you from the moment I knew you were real, and I will love you until my last breath. I have absolutely no doubt that I will see you in heaven and that in death, as in life, the three of you will teach me more lessons than I could possibly imagine. I am so fortunate to have had you for the short time that I did. I love you, and I'm proud to be your mama.

# Healing

It is February 19, 2013. Two years ago yesterday, I lost one of my babies. It was the baby that I was farthest along with and, to this day, the one that causes me the most pain. It was this baby—lost in February, due in October—that began my spiral down into depression.

One year ago yesterday, I sat alone at home, in a bathtub, prepared to end my life. My main reason for not following through with it was my family and, perhaps not coincidentally, the children in my life who were too young and innocent to be touched by such a tragedy as suicide.

I realized yesterday that the date, February 18, 2013, is far more symbolic than just an anniversary. It was 2/18/13. We found out we were pregnant on the second, lost our baby on the eighteenth, and it was due to be born on the thirteenth. Somehow, these numbers are connected. They have meaning in our future; of this I have no doubt.

As yesterday's date approached, I was thinking about the last two years of my life. The first year after the miscarriage is essentially lost to time now. I don't remember most of it. It's funny how you don't realize you are simply existing until you start to actually live again. The second year was one of healing. I'll never be completely healed, but I started to become myself again—maybe even a better self. I am stronger now; that is for certain.

Jalal ad-Din Muhammad Rumi was a 13th-century Persian poet and theologian, who once said, "The wound is the place where the light enters you."

This couldn't be truer for me. I was wounded. For a while I didn't know whether I would survive the wound. But while I was fighting to survive, the light was entering me without my knowledge. The light is the reason why today I am able to look forward to what the future will bring. The light is the love that surrounds me, the strength I gained, and the person I am proud that I've become.

I would like to stop writing this now. It's not because the journey is over. It is a journey that I will be taking my entire life. And it's not because I want to forget. I will remember my babies forever. After all, the only place they ever truly existed was inside of me, so it is my duty to remember them. I would like to stop writing because I am ready for the closure that it will bring. I am ready to move on with the next stage of our journey to become a family.

One thing is for certain: no matter what the next stage may bring, I will never forget our beautiful babies dear.